VINCENT GIGANTE BIOGRAPHY

The Inside Story of the Mafia's Eccentric Boss Who Ruled New York's Underworld While Pretending to Be Crazy

Blake Hayden

Table Of Contents

His parents had immigrated to America, like many others of their age, with hopes for success and a better life for their offspring.

The difficulties of being an immigrant were directly experienced by young Vincent as he grew up on the Lower East Side's busy streets. The area was a melting pot of ambitions and difficulties, brimming with a variety of cultures.

In this hardscrabble setting, Gigante learned the value of loyalty, family, and community—lessons he would take with him into the criminal underworld.

Early Signs of Trouble

There were early indications that Vincent Gigante was not meant to follow the typical route. He was lured to the streets, where he met friends among his contemporaries, many of whom were already dabbling in petty crimes.

For a young and naïve Gigante, it was impossible to resist the pull of the street life with its fast money and promise of power.

The criminal scene in New York City underwent a major upheaval when Vincent Gigante reached adulthood.

One of the Five Families that would eventually control the underbelly of the city, the Genovese criminal family, was only starting. Vito Genovese, the founder of the family, was creating an empire based on immorality, brutality, and the omertà, or holy pledge of silence.

Chapter 2

The Ascendance of "The Chin"

It's impossible to overstate how impressive Vincent "The Chin" Gigante's rise in the world of organized crime was.

From his lowly origins on the Lower East Side, he would ascend to become an important member of the Genovese crime family, which would ultimately have a disproportionate amount of control over the city's criminal underbelly.

Gigante's rise through the Genovese criminal family's ranks was characterized by a mix of cunning and brutality. He was someone who appreciated the virtue of patience and knew when to act quickly and when to take his time.

Gigante tended to work in the background, allowing others to have their attention while he planned his next move, in contrast to some of his contemporaries who were flashier and more flamboyant.

Gigante found himself negotiating a complicated web of allegiances and conflicts inside the Genovese criminal family.

With Vito Genovese in charge, the family was run like a well-oiled machine. Gigante was a respected and imposing personality who quietly accumulated power and influence, while not being in the limelight.

Alliances might be formed and destroyed quickly in the world of organized crime. Rival families fought for control of lucrative criminal operations and areas, and alliances were often just as flimsy as they were tactical.

Chapter 4
The Mob's Silent Kingpin

Vincent "The Chin" Gigante was a conundrum in the secret lanes of organized crime. His function inside the Genovese criminal family is unclear because of his erratic personality and propensity to come seem mentally ill.

However, this mask covered a man with extraordinary authority and cunning—a quiet kingpin whose power went well beyond his mysterious act.

The impact Gigante had on the criminal underground extended well beyond the show he put on for the public. He was a strategist when no one was looking, carefully planning the Genovese family's actions.

His reserved attitude belied his firm control over the affairs of the family, making him a formidable opponent.

The fact that Gigante was involved in so many unlawful businesses was evidence of his adaptability as a criminal genius. He had an excellent eye for possibilities, which he ruthlessly took advantage of.

Gigante's influence reached into every nook and cranny of the criminal underworld in New York City, from illicit gambling dens that generated millions in revenue to labor unions that he infiltrated and controlled.

The Genovese criminal family reigned supreme in the Big Apple for a while under Gigante's direction. They had control over a wide range of criminal activity, including extortion, drug trafficking, and murder for hire.

They had access to the most powerful members of New York City's political and financial elite, which gave them freedom to act without consequence.

Gigante nonetheless faced various difficulties and dangers despite his might and influence. His leadership was put to the test by the ongoing battles between rival criminal organizations over rich territory.

His kingdom was always in danger as law enforcement, which was always on the lookout, tried to figure out the enigma surrounding his mental condition.

Chapter 5

The Personal Cost of the Act

There was a rich personal world populated by complex relationships, sacrifices, and betrayals hidden under Vincent "The Chin" Gigante's quirkiness and the façade of organized criminal dominance.

In sharp contrast to the reputation he worked so hard to build, Vincent Gigante's private life was a conundrum.

He was a spouse, a parent, and a friend while operating in the shadows of the criminal underground. But the persistent fear of violence and the ominous specter of treachery often cast a shadow over this private existence.

Loyalty was valued inside the Genovese criminal family but was also seen as a possible flaw. Trust was hard to earn and simple to lose. Gigante was not immune to betrayals despite his diligent cultivation of devotion.

Rival sections within the family attempted to overthrow his leadership, resulting in fatal clashes that endangered the unity of the unit.

Due to his leadership role within the Genovese family, Gigante was the subject of multiple assassination attempts. His enemies included other mobsters, police enforcement, and even members of his own family. As a continual reminder of the dangerous world he lived in, the possibility of violence hovered over him like an ominous cloud.

The Genovese family was increasingly under the control of Gigante, and with that growth came an increase in violence and dread.

His criminal activities, which ranged from illicit gambling to labor racketeering, made an impression on New York City's neighborhoods and commercial establishments. His activities had a ripple effect throughout society, hurting both innocent and complicit people.

Chapter 6
The Puzzle

Few people in the history of organized crime have remained as elusive and mysterious as Vincent "The Chin" Gigante. Gigante's actual identity was a conundrum that law enforcement agencies were fervently trying to solve as they sought the guy hiding behind the quirky façade.

The law enforcement organizations entrusted with prosecuting Vincent Gigante had to deal with a strong foe.

Investigators found it difficult to discern between reality and fiction because of his odd conduct, which had generated an atmosphere of impenetrability.

However, the authorities remained steadfast as more corpses accumulated and the Genovese family's criminal enterprise grew.

The attempted murder of gangster Frank Costello was a turning point in Gigante's rise to prominence. As a result of the attack's power vacuum, Gigante was able to advance inside the Genovese family.

It was a turning point in his criminal career, one that had repercussions for the family and police enforcement alike.

In their tenacious pursuit of Gigante, law enforcement authorities used wiretaps and surveillance in tandem. They eavesdropped on talks, kept an eye on his whereabouts, and collected proof of his participation in illegal actions.

Gigante's legal team presented a strong defense, contending that he was mentally ill to stand trial, but the subsequent court fights proved to be a substantial barrier.

One of the most momentous court battles in the history of organized crime would be the trial of Vincent Gigante. It was a war of wits as prosecutors tried to expose the many layers of fabrication that had long covered Gigante.

The trial eventually revealed "The Chin" as the vicious mafia leader he was, who had meticulously planned out a criminal empire.

Chapter 7
Gigante's Legacy

The world of organized crime and the metropolis that served as its background had both been forever changed by Vincent "The Chin" Gigante's rule.

Cunning, ruthlessness and a mastery of deceit were characteristics of Gigante's leadership of the Genovese crime family. His tenure had a lasting impact on the corporation, and his influence permeated every aspect of the family's business.

His legacy includes a vast enterprise with ties to the criminal underbelly of New York City, including illicit gambling, labor unions, and extortion.

The collapse of "The Chin" resulted in several seismic changes inside the New York Mafia. Other crime families looked to take advantage of the power vacuum as the Genovese family struggled to deal with the fallout from his arrest and sentencing.

This time of change and unpredictability would be pivotal in the development of organized crime in the city.

The public's fascination with Vincent Gigante's peculiarity dates back many decades. His dual existence as a violent mafia leader and a guy who seemed to be mentally deranged led to a mystique that persisted long after his incarceration. Numerous myths and stories about "The Oddfather"'s life have remained because they were fascinated with him.

Hollywood, which has always been fascinated by gangster and mafia life, has its interpretation of Vincent Gigante's tale. Filmmakers have plenty of material to work with thanks to his mysterious personality and the mystery surrounding his criminal history

Vincent Gigante's criminal organization left a permanent mark on New York City.

The effects of organized crime were still being felt in the communities and companies he had affected. Even when his rule came to an end, the effects of his deeds were felt across society.

Chapter 8
The Underworld

As the mystery surrounding Vincent "The Chin" Gigante's reputation faded, organized crime in New York City continued to develop. In the years after Gigante, organized crime in New York City saw several notable transformations. The criminal scene had changed, and new players had appeared.

The city's criminal underground has evolved to meet new possibilities and difficulties, transitioning from conventional Italian-American mafia families to a more varied assortment of criminal groups.

Following Gigante's demise, the Genovese crime family was at a turning point. It was a period of reflection and adjustment. Since Vincent Gigante's time in power, New York City has seen significant change.

The environment in which organized crime functioned had been changed by changes in the economy, urban growth, and law enforcement initiatives

The actions and strategies of Vincent Gigante provided insightful information on the world of organized crime.

As we wrap off our exploration of Vincent Gigante's life and times by looking at the state of organized crime in New York City today. The story of organized crime in New York City is ever-evolving, shaped by its past but always looking toward the future.

In the end, Vincent Gigante's tale serves as a reminder of organized crime's enduring appeal and dynamic character. It serves as a sobering reminder of the lasting power of deception and the intricate legacy one person may create in the shady realm of illegal activity.

Printed in Great Britain
by Amazon

33228022R00015